Source-based Questions At A-Level

by JOHN FINES

THE HISTORICAL ASSOCIATION
59a Kennington Park Road, London SE11 4JH

Acknowledgements

We reproduce the extracts and illustrations listed below by kind permission of:

pages 16, 19, 21, 22, 27, 32, 41, 43, Berkshire Record Office; *page 17* Lincolnshire Record Office; *page 20* Bodleian Library; *page 23* Northern Ireland Public Record Office; *page 25* The Trustees of the Goodwood Collection; *page 30* Worcester Record Office; *page 31* British Rail, Western Region; *page 38* The Times and the Trustees of the Royal Hampshire Regiment Museum; *page 42* The Wall Street Journal; *page 45* Margaret Bourke White/Life (c) Time Inc.

ISBN 0 85278 267 5

HA 1.8.84

Originated and published by The Historical Association, 59a Kennington Park Road, London SE11 4JH and printed in Great Britain by The Chameleon Press Limited, 5-25 Burr Road, London SW18 4SG

Contents

Contents

Source-based Questions

Source-based questions have been with us for a long time, at both O- and A-levels, as well as in CSE (where, particularly in the Southern Region Examinations Board (SREB) Paper 2 for the Schools' Council Project History, by far the most advanced level of thinking about examining in History has taken place). Nearly all boards at A-level already use source-based questions, and the Joint Matriculation Board (JMB) and Associated Examining Board (AEB) (particularly in its Pilot Project Scheme) have done much to advance the extensive use of this method. Recently the deliberations on the *Common Core at A-level* agreed to recommend that their objective (b) should receive at least 20% of the total marks: 'to test the candidates'...ability to evaluate and interpret source material as historical evidence and to demonstrate facility in its use'. So we shall be in future testing evaluation, interpretation and use of sources.

But what are **sources** and how may one use them? The Common Core document uses terms like **document question** and **evidence question** in addition to the term sources, and one suspects that a long history of disagreement about this type of question has not yet reached resolution. The confusion revolves largely around the use of terminology and this needs sorting out a little. It is most important in the first place to see sources as wide ranging – the historian may use statistics or aerial photographs as readily as yellowing pieces of paper covered with ancient script. Thus we should more readily use the term **source** than the term **document**, reserving the latter for a complete item of primary material in continuous prose. Similarly it is vital to recall that **evidence** is what historians get out of sources for their own use – sources cannot be seen as evidence until evidence is found in them and put to specifically historical uses.

Stimulus Material

Some of the earliest source-based questions appeared under the strange title of **stimulus material**, and the use of this term persists – in current literature Northern Ireland and Cambridge both issue guides to the creation of stimulus material questions (the latter relating to O-level, however). The theory of stimulus material questions was never very fully worked out, but the idea seems to have been that the pupils looked at the piece of documentation (more often than not, for some strange reason, a *Punch* cartoon) and drew interest from it in answering questions that were in fact largely similar to all the other questions on the paper, in that they tested factual recall more than engaging the candidate in any major enquiry into the material in itself. This is not to say that stimulus response questions must always be bad. The idea of finding interest in a source is central to the historical process, but it does require careful questioning to draw out a response that will use that interest to demonstrate the student's powers of thinking, as against mere conditioned responses of a formal order.

The Gobbet

The second main stream in source questions is the **gobbet** question. Like so much in Advanced level examining, this is a hang-over from university style questioning, especially in third year special subject papers. The candidates are expected to study a prescribed range of documentation, and are tested afterwards simply to determine that they have done so. Of course, gobbet questions can do much more than this (for example, they can ask questions about the provenance of the document and about its context in general that are less easy to ask of unseen sources), but they must be largely structured by the **intention** of the gobbet style itself. Some boards are particularly keen on this approach, and Oxford (notable for its publications to aid teachers and students understand what the board is requiring from them) publishes a guide to answering gobbet questions. The gobbet style is overtly rejected by a number of boards, but there is a hang-over effect here too, for boards are publishing or even commissioning as well as recommending already published exemplar collections of documents for student use in preparation for the examination. Whilst this is a perfectly understandable and in most cases thoroughly commendable action, we should be aware that sets of exemplars may move the examining back in the direction of old-style gobbets.

The Material Used

The third element in the argument that underlies source questioning is the seen/unseen, course-related/unrelated argument. Most boards and indeed most teachers would go for the unseen but related answer in this argument, that is, they want documents candidates will not have met before (although they will be familiar with their type and style) and they want these documents to relate to the course studied in terms of period and topic. Some examiners at A-level throw up their hands in horror at the deliberately unrelated nature of the documentation examined in the Schools' Council Project History 13-16 Paper 2. The exception that must be mentioned here is the AEB pilot scheme: for some years now pupils have faced one of their papers in which half the time and a third of the marks are accorded to an exercise on unseen and unrelated documents. Four documents or clusters of documents are presented for choice on the part of the pupil. The examiners obviously regard the choice of documents on which to comment as very much the pupil's privilege, for despite some criticism they have kept this element of choice, on teacher advice as well as from their own convictions.

Reading Problems

There are two types of reading problem in this exercise: first there is a language problem about the extracts themselves, if chosen from an ancient or unusual source (thus medieval wills foxed some candidates recently, and one suspects the use of extracts from plays or poems might be unexpected too). The second problem is simply that of length, for many of these documents or groups of documents are long. One might suspect, however, that the demand to read concentrates the mind and and the attention quite well: it is the short essay questions which the pupil hastily scans and so misreads that leads to irrelevance in answers. Such evidence as we have from this and other boards suggests that the document questions are popular with pupils and they gain relatively high marks on them (although there is a tendency towards a superficial response to the surface of the words, rather than a deep questioning of what lies beneath the language, the unwitting evidence the document presents). One interesting suggestion has been scouted for a different format for document-based examinations that might help out with difficulties: the six hour practical, in which students would receive a clutch of documents from which to answer a given question. This strikes one as a most interesting idea that should be examined further, because it allows the time that an answer in depth requires, and sets up more realistic circumstances in which the enterprise of 'being an historian', for the time being, may be undertaken.

Finding the Sources

Obviously all these forms of examining are costly, and many boards are worried at the problem of finding enough sources to use, especially when one is looking for documents which give a strongly contrasting picture. Banks will need to be established, and Record Offices combed for materials. There is no true shortage of documents, the problem is finding the questions to be asked about them. In this respect the AEB scheme seems to be able to put quite a wide range of types of question. The most used formats seem to be questions of evaluation and judgement (what is the use of this extract, how may one rely on it in use?) but there are also interesting questions on the balanced judgement of documents, involving a more refined critique of sources, on straightforward analysis, synthesis and comparison, and, be it noted, high order comprehension questions. It is a conventional mistake to assume that all comprehension questions are lowly (e.g. 'What clues does Document D contain as to the character, aims and power of other members of the Convention and of the Convention as a whole?' is very high order comprehension indeed). One last point worthy of note is that the examiners try, over a sequence of papers to set questions on a wide range of skills – commendable in itself, no doubt, but leaving teacher

and pupil in some doubt as to what is to be tested **this** year – the Pilot
Scheme has its own conventionalities!

We should be aware that there are a number of types of questions that
are dangerous because they are foolish and non-productive in
education. We would all agree that questions about documents *should*
be about understanding, and that this may only be checked in use, with
some active translation of the material. In fact we often ask idiotic
questions, which do no good at all. In my book there are four categories
of idiotic questions:

1   The 'wake up at the back there' type: who went across the road?
    When did Charles wake up? What did Sherman do in response? All
    that these questions require of children is that they should find the
    right line in the passage and read off the response. This bastardises
    the whole notion of asking questions and teaches children that
    questions are stupid and meaningless; it suggests that the whole
    passage is of no value, and only the line that holds the answer is of
    any worth. These questions are *constantly* asked and should always
    be branded for what they are.

2   The 'secret question' type, whereby a simple request for a definition
    is an excuse to ask for more knowledge. This is (even more than
    Type 1) a signal to children that the exercise is not only potty, but
    also deeply unfair. When a child reads 'Who was the "Sun King"
    referred to on line 14 and why was he so called?' he recognises that
    the examiner is going to reward conventional knowledge, not an
    interpretation of the document itself. These questions are insidious
    and creep into papers unawares.

3   The 'nudge, nudge, wink, wink' type of question, whereby the setter
    is hoping for a similar response to the document that he has had, but
    only in the slightest manner will he signal what he really means. It is
    as in the classroom where the teacher often gives out a question
    which ought to be prefixed with the instruction 'Now, I want you all
    to read my mind...'. Such questions come out on paper mostly in the
    form 'do you find anything strange/interesting about the statement
    on line 43?'.

Finally, I must put in what I call the 'imagine you are a badger' type of
question. Here the children are faced with a totally impossible
imaginative (or empathetic) task, and the examiner sits back confident
that few will answer, but those who do will provide a good laugh.

So rarely do we get a good question, the one that makes a straight
proposition: there is a problem about this document, and this is it. To
deal with it, we must do these things. Do them. What are your findings?

Responses to the Common Core

It is important at this stage to comment briefly on the first two responses
to the Common Core paper – those of the AEB and Cambridge, to see
what they have to say on the subject. Both these responses have been

very speedy, but rely on development work in the two boards that long preceded the meetings of the Common Core Committee.

The Associated Examining Board

The AEB have decided to restrict the document questions to the new Depth paper in their History examination (replacing the old Special Subject paper). They have there two compulsory questions, one on a single source, and one on a group (thus resolving the argument of which format is best rather neatly, but still side-stepping that issue!). The sources are unseen items, related to the topic, and may be of all kinds, including secondary sources. In Economic and Social History there is to be one question on statistical sources, in addition to the document question and one question on the methodology of history. In the sample papers it seems that the level of questioning is lower than that used in the pilot scheme, with stronger emphasis on simple comprehension and the use of general knowledge of the topic (definiton of terms, old favourite in document questions, might well bulk large in this scheme). The AEB presentation is still at a stage of discussion, so may not be adjudicated upon, but it does raise a number of interesting points which contrast with the solutions arrived at by the Cambridge Board, which has now received Schools' Council approval.

The Cambridge Board

Cambridge will set a compulsory document question in both outline and special subject papers. In the outline paper this commitment has forced upon the examination an interesting, and highly commendable development, for the board will declare the topic on which the document will be set, and will issue a syllabus for this topic. Thus we will have a syllabus within a syllabus, and a following of the lead given by JMB in declaring topics to be assessed. Oxford Board's plans, recently issued, follow closely the Cambridge pattern with declared topics for source-based questions and only primary sources being used. There is also a recommendation to study methodological texts. Their questions will, however, be on the outline paper, an interesting choice. In addition they daringly offer specimen answers to their own specimen questions.

Cambridge (like most of the other boards) is somewhat defensive on the topic of disaggregating marks for skills, and claims this cannot be done in the same breath as admitting that teachers may well teach skills separately! But it does make a good job of listing what it is looking for, and what it will **not** be doing. Candidates are asked to explain, to compare, to judge reliability and usefulness both internally and externally, and to test assertions by reference to the document. The board will not ask for copying or precis of the document, vapid speculation, questions simply requiring knowledge not in the document, generalised, unguided assessment or particular assessment of authenticity.

In its very full statement about the way it intends to handle documents the board is to be commended, but not necessarily agreed with, and there are many issues to be raised. Not least one may question their decisions about the sources to be used themselves: these will be contemporary written records, not in any circumstances secondary sources, or, it seems, primary sources of any other kind. These written records will be short, modernised and glossed. There will be more than one, suggesting a strong bid for comparison and contrast.

However one may argue philosophically with the decisions of the boards, at least Cambridge (and AEB when it comes to final format) is making itself clear to teachers about what it is doing. My own critique revolves around the extent and the thoroughness of the testing of skills proposed. Do the tests as indicated provide an adequate experience of the historian's use of documents? Do the marking arrangements suggest a clear reward for achievement at the right level? In response to this second question one should point once more to the SREB's achievements in establishing hierarchies of levels of achievement related both to the skills to be tested in the question and to pupil performance in that particular examination. This kind of marking may be costly in its initial stages of development, but no one can deny that it can be done.

The Range of Skills Tested

In order to itemise the range of skills to be tested if one is to cover the whole area of the historical experience it is necessary to set up some sort of checklist, rather than the more general statements of acceptable questioning issued by the boards. It is, of course, perfectly possible to turn a checklist of skills into a typology of questions, and achieve both goals. To provide such a list I unashamedly turn back to the *Educational Objectives for the Study of History: a suggested framework* (Historical Association, Teaching of History series 35, 1971), which I compiled with Dr Coltham so long ago. I have said before how regularly I myself use this document, despite all sorts of reservations and developments in my own thinking, and I do find it very useful in this case. I shall not be using its format, but will reformulate under three relatively handy headings: questions relating to handling (processing) evidence, questions relating to evaluation and questions relating to the application of the evidence. In each case I will try to formulate the type of question that might be set, but do not at this stage apply it to specific forms of evidence.

Handling of Evidence
1   Questions about the **nature** of the source: what kind of document is this? Does its form define it in any special way?
2   Questions about **circumstances**: who wrote this document, under what pressures, for what purpose, when, to whom, where, etc?

3   Questions about **knowledge**: what else would we need to know to interpret this document fully? What knowledge **might** exist somewhere that we could draw upon to aid us?

4   Questions about **analysis**: how many different parts are there in this document, and how might we regroup them? How are they related to one another within the body of the source itself?

5   Questions about **translation**: could we put this evidence into another more convenient form, so that we could see it more clearly, understand it better?

6   Questions about **concepts**: can you isolate, describe and name the concepts used in this document and its interpretation (including larger concepts such as continuity/change, cause/effect)?

7   Questions about **relevance**: having analysed, can you sort out which parts are relevant to what topic?

8   Questions about **period**: can you apply period and time sense to this source – can you empathise in a properly detached way, can you visualise both the time and conditions?

Evaluation of Sources

1   Questions about **authenticity** (*pace* Cambridge!): on what criteria might we be able to use this piece of evidence? What questions would you want to ask of it before using it? One may of course formulate questions about provenance without being in a position to answer them in an examination room.

2   Questions about **consistency**: is this source all of a piece, does it contradict itself in any way? Does it seem to disagree with other evidences? (Multiple sources may, of course, be specifically compared under this heading, but they are not absolutely necessary for this exercise.)

3   Questions about **completeness**: are there any gaps here? What might it have told us, what might we have expected to find in it?

4   Questions about **credibility**: does our common sense make us tend to suspect or believe it, and why? Can common sense lead us anywhere with this document?

5   Questions of **judgement**: what point of view is being expressed here? Are there unstated assumptions? Does it contain value-judgements? Is there evidence of bias, and is it intended or unintended, conscious or unconscious?

Application

1   Can you sort out what **questions** the source raises, as well as the answer it gives?

2   Can you estimate the **significance** of the evidence?

3   Can you **extrapolate** from the evidence to provide a conclusion, or an hypothesis? (Of course the question might supply an hypothesis to be applied, but this would be a lower order test.)

4   Can you provide a **description,** a **comparison** or an **interpretation** as
    a result of using the evidence that conforms to the pattern of what
    we call history?

The above list is only a beginning, and is full of holes, quite apart from
being untested. What it does suggest, however, is that there is a range of
questions to be applied to sources, a wide one.

A SELECTION
OF
SOURCES

TABLE 1. THE SOURCES LISTED

1 Escape of a Murderer, 1506;	8 Northern Ireland, 1798;	15 The Victoria Cross;	
2 Costs of the Reformation;	9 Swing Letter, 1830;	16 The Water Bottle, 1880;	
3 A Policy on Gypsies, 1537	10 House Plan;	17 Letter about an Airman, 1916;	
4 A Broker's Suggestions, 1614;	11 Rough Music, 1839;	18 A Welcome for Mussolini, 1923;	
5 Doodles in the Cabinet;	12 Train Times,	19 The General Strike;	
6 A Holiday Booking, 1776;	13 The Poacher, 1847;	20 A Family Portrait	
7 The Cost of Living, 1775;	14 Slavery Observed, 1853;		

TABLE 2. The Sources and the Skills

Skills	Sources																			
	1	2	3	4	5	6	7	8	9	10	11	12	13	14	15	16	17	18	19	20
Handling			✓	✓	✓			✓	✓		✓	✓		✓	✓	✓	✓	✓	✓	✓
			✓	✓	✓	✓	✓	✓	✓		✓	✓		✓	✓		✓	✓	✓	✓
	✓					✓	✓	✓	✓	✓	✓	✓	✓			✓				✓
	✓										✓	✓	✓		✓				✓	✓
	✓		✓	✓		✓	✓	✓	✓	✓	✓	✓		✓		✓		✓	✓	✓
	✓		✓	✓		✓	✓	✓	✓	✓	✓	✓		✓	✓	✓	✓	✓	✓	✓
Evaluation					✓						✓				✓	✓		✓		✓
											✓			✓				✓	✓	✓
					✓			✓	✓	✓	✓	✓		✓	✓		✓	✓	✓	✓
			✓					✓	✓	✓	✓	✓		✓	✓	✓	✓	✓	✓	✓
Application	✓	✓	✓			✓		✓	✓	✓	✓	✓	✓	✓	✓	✓	✓	✓	✓	✓
	✓	✓	✓			✓	✓	✓	✓	✓	✓	✓	✓	✓	✓	✓		✓	✓	✓
		✓	✓						✓		✓	✓	✓						✓	✓
	✓	✓				✓	✓	✓	✓	✓	✓	✓	✓	✓	✓	✓	✓	✓	✓	✓

A Selection of Sources

Opposite is the selection of sources presented for classroom practice in this pamphlet together with the list of skills required. It has been made on a number of grounds. In the first place I have tried to provide interesting documents with interesting things to to with them. Alas this is not always possible in the examination room, but because the source questions in examinations are sometimes less than interesting there is no reason why the practical experience leading up to the examination should be boring. Secondly, the sources have been chosen for their accessibility, from newspaper cuttings, from record office collections; it is hoped that will demonstrate to all teachers (and to all examiners) that there is no shortage of readily available materials. Of course this does mean that the collection here is largely of private and often parochial materials, rather than from public and international documentation. This certainly doesn't invalidate it as practice materials, and does aid our first intention of keeping the material interesting. Thirdly, the sources are chosen and questions set on them to illustrate the application of the typology of questions given above. The relationship of the source questions to the typology is shown in Table 2 which will aid the teacher who is anxious to find sources to use when concentrating on particular areas of skill. Fourthly, the sources have been chosen with more flexibility than is allowed to an examiner. Some reading difiiculties are left for pupils to cope with, because this is a natural part of the historian's experience with sources and in the classroom (as distinct from the examination room) there is time to cope with these.

In tackling the sources, especially the more complex or the lengthier documents, the teacher and students should be aware of the values of learning to read such materials efficiently and easily. First one must be aware of what one is reading for, and the question should give some hint of that. However open ended the question might seem, it will indicate what one is intended to search for in the source.
Indeed it is this business of searching, rather than reading as such, that needs encouraging in the students. A line by line reading is often less than helpful – a stumbling experience that deflates the ego and destroys the power to memorise or analyse on the way. Much better to scan for evidence: recently, for example, I used source 4 with a group of sixth formers who found it at first glance very off putting indeed. So I split up the reading task for them. First I asked only for a biographical information – anything the document said about characters, so that we could set up a cast list. I gave only a few minutes for this exercise and it was creditably carried out. I then asked for geographical information and gave another few minutes for the search, following it with a request for chronological information – material about dates. By now the students had scanned their way through the document at least three times and were very familiar with it. At this stage they could be asked about the nature and significance of the evidence to be found within it.

1. Escape of a Murderer, 1506

The following document comes from the year 1506, and survives in the Berkshire Record Office (W/JBc 35). It is given as written, and presents some problems to the reader. If you were to use it in an historical work (say an essay on sanctuary) you would need to give a brief but thorough account of its contents. Try your hand at this job, and add a comment on sanctuary. Why do you think going into Oxfordshire seems so important?

Richard Morgan servaunt in the priory of Walyngford hath confessid by fore mayster mayre of Walyngford, John humson and Thomas Jenyns and Thomas Polehampton & John Richardson beyng present in the Castell of Walyngford in the xxiii^d daye of Novembre in the xxii^d yere of our kyng harry the viith, that Robert Ford late beyng in sanctuary in the priory of Walyngford for the murder of Sir John Skeffeld prieste, the seid Richard seith that the seid Robert Forde was conveyid oute of the seid priory the Wednysday nyght or Thursdaye nyght next by fore Whitesonday last passed by twene x and xi of the clocke in the nyght; upon the which the seid Richard seith that Dane William hymyngford munke of the seid place came at the seide oure by fore wreton, to Thomas dybbedon & Tomas martyne and to the seid Richard Morgan, servauntes all in the seid priory, desirying and prayng them to helpe conveye the seide Robert Forde owte fro the seid priory to the sanctuary to Culham in Oxforde shire The seid W hemynford munke and the seid Robert Forde comyng to geder meetyng at a postern gate with the seid iii servaunts And then they went alforth to geder in to the olde Culham howse garden and there the seide monke seid sirres goe ye forth and god be youre goode spede / And so he departid fro them agen / And then they servaunts wente forth with the seid murdere Robert Ford to a path by the blake darke with in the precinktes of the priory foreseid And there they wente over to Culham warde to a folde next by the hondy & crosse, metyng there with Richard Ford the son of John Forde and ii other persones the which I know not there names, by the poynetement of the fore seid munke and the seid Richard Forde there to mete at the seide Folde / And then we were vi personnes by sides the seid murderer / And then we all wende forth to geder to a wotter side; the seide murderer callid for a bote and within a littel space came a man with a bote and received the foreseid Robert Forde in to the bote and none of al the partie wende no ferther forth. And the boteman seide that he wulde bryng the murderer in to savegarde within the space of ii owris. And so we all departid comming home warde (Dorso) Ayen to the howse of John ffordes And there we did ete and drinke and departid every man his way.

2. Costs of the Reformation

The following extracts are taken from the Churchwardens' accounts of Leverton, near Boston in Lincolnshire. How might they help an historian to write about the effect of the various changes in religion upon the common man? (Volume of Accounts, 1492-1625, deposited in the Lincolnshire Archives Office.)

1526: 'Recevyd of Janet ffranckyshe for the legacye of William ffranckyshe hyr husband to the biynge of ymages of Alybaster to be set in the foresyde of the rode lofite: xlvi^s viii^d'

1549: 'Item payd to the peintor for penntyng over the Rod loft: iii^s viii^d'

1555: 'payd to John lynne for a pyxe: vii^s viii^d'

1561: 'item paid for removynge the Alters out of the chyrch: xiii^d'

3. A Policy on Gypsies, 1537

The following letter was written by the King's principal officer to the Earl of Chester in 1537. It is taken from Henry Ellis's Original Letter, First Series, Vol 2, pp. 100-103. *How might it be used by an historian specially concerned with Hitler's racial policies?*

After my right hartie commendations. Whereas the Kings Majestie, about a twelfmoneth past, gave a pardonne to a company of lewde [ignorant, unlearned] personnes within this realme calling themselves Gipcyans, for a most shamfull and detestable murder commytted amongs them, with speceall proviso inserted by their owne consents, that onles they shuld all avoyde this his Graces realme by a certeyn daye long sythens expired, yt shuld be lawfull to all his Graces offycers to hang them all in places of his realme, where they myght be apprehended, without any further examynacion or tryal after forme of the lawe, as in their letter patents of the said pardon is expressed. His Grace, hering tell that they doo yet lynger here within his realme, not avoyding the same according to his commaundement and their owne promes, and that albeit his poore subjects be dayly spoyled, robbed and deceyved by them, yet his Highnes officers and Ministres lytle regarding their dieuties towards his Majestye, do permyt them to lynger and loyter in all partys, and to exercise all their falshods, felonyes and treasons unpunished, hathe commaunded me to sygnifye unto youe, and the Shires next adjoynyng, whether any of the sayd personnes called themselfes Egipcyans, or that hathe heretofore called themselfes Egipcyans, shall fortune to enter or travayle in the same. And in cace youe shall here or knowe of any suche, be they men or women, that ye shall compell them to depart to the next porte of the See to the place where they shalbe taken, and eyther wythout delaye uppon the first wynde that may conveye them into any parte of beyond the Sees, to take shipping and to passe in to owtward partyes, or if they shall in any wise breke that commaundement, without any tract [stay, hesitation] to see them executed according to the Kings Hieghnes sayd Lettres patents remaynyng of Recorde in his Chauncery which, with these, shalbe your discharge in that behaulf: not fayling taccomplishe the tenor hereof with all effect and diligence, without sparing uppon any Commyssion, Licence, or Placarde that they may shewe or aledge for themselfes to the contrary, as ye tender his Graces pleasor which also ys that youe shall gyve notyce toall the Justices of the Peax in that Countye where youe resyde, and the Shires adjoynant, that they may accomplishe the tenor hereof accordingly. Thus far ye hertely wel; From the Neate the vth day of December the xxix[th] yer of his Ma[ties]
Most noble Regne
Yo[r] louyng ffreend
THOMAS CRUMWELL
To my verye good Lorde my Lorde of
Chestre President of the Marches of Wales

4. A Broker's Suggestion, 1614

Read the following letter to Sir Nicholas Carew at Beddingfield (Berkshire Record Office D/ELl C1/44). What do you think is the writer's occupation? What does the document suggest about the way the gentry of this period preserved and expanded their positions?

Right worshipful sir,

I pray let it not seme strange that I presume to wright thes ffewe lynes, for I doe it out of my love, to certefy you of a besines that was moved by a gentelman – a frind of myne – unto my selfe concerninge an Intent of a mocyon to ben made to Mr. Chaunclour of the Exchequer about a gentelwoman a wedowe in Warwicksher; but with this Causion that if he had Ever a daughtour under the age of 15 yeares to be had withe a good porcyon for hir sune, that is as yet but 15 yeares of age, that then the widowe would be the willinger to treat of a match, both for hurselfe, and for hur sune. The livinge to the younge man is 800 or neare 1000 p.annum, but the mother will howld a good part during hur lyfe. A very goodly howse in the mydst of the lande 4 myles from Covintry. To lay downe what is confydently Reaported of the Lady and hur sune is this: first the gentelwoman is neare 40 yeares of age, very vertuous and Relegyonly given, personuble, welfavoured fayer and of that excelent carage & behaviour as Rare to fynd a matche; hur Sune a ffine younge man: well applyed to his bookes. And the porcyon that she desirs with him being 25 or 30ᵉ poundes though 2 or 3 yeares a paying will Cleare all other legases & deptes what soever; so that if your selfe shuld have a daughtor of ffittinge yeares as I suppos you have and a disposesecyon to harken to such a mocyon as this, then happely you may have at one a good match bothe for yourselfe and your daughtour together, and the land to followe your daughtour in a large manor for a Joyntour and to hur Heyours if god bles them with any; and the whole living to yourselfe present if you please to harcken to suche a motion as thes. I can at any time bringe you to confering withe a gentelman, one Mr Egerton, hur kindsman who cane cartefy all things more at lardge. I am the rather thus bowld with your woship for that I knowe thes thinges doe sumtimes happen very strangly; yet altogether by the great providenc of god; and my self withe in this 2 munthes hane bine the Author to bring a gentelman by Reding and Sir Thomas Cuttelers daughtor to gether which never hurde on of the other before, and had in porcyon 3 thousand poundes. If you please to harken then I pray sir within 7 dayes let me heare from your worship, if not I shale suppose the mocyon dyes. So wishing you muche prosperytie I take leave and rest at your worships servis.

EDMOND WOLFERSTON

Colmanstret the 1 Octobre 1614.

5. Doodle in the Cabinet

These notes are taken from Bodleian Library Ms Clarendon 100 f. 54. It appears that King Charles II and his chief minister Clarendon exchanged notes during a particularly boring meeting in council. What light do they cast on the relationship of these two? When you have written what you have to say, find out more by reading about the relationship, and see whether your judgement stands up, or needs further consideration.

'I would willingly make a visite to may sister at tunbridge for a night or two at farthest, when do you thinke I can best spare that time?'

'I know no reason why you may not for such a tyme (2 nights) go the next weeke, about Wensday or Thursday, and returne tyme enough for the adjournement: which yett ought to be the weeke followinge.
    I suppose you will goe with a light Trayne.'

'I intend to take nothing but my night bag.'

'God, you will not go without 40 or 50 horse?' [this last in another hand]

'I counte that parte of my night bag.'

6. A Holiday Booking, 1766

This draft letter asking for rooms at Bath is preserved in the Berkshire Record Office (D/EHy F83). What light does it cast upon the condition of late eighteenth century gentry?

London April 10 1766

Mr Stennet

Some very particular friends of ours whom you must know by name (Sir George Saville's sister Mrs Hewitt and family) are coming to Bath. We should be much obliged to you if you would lookout for Lodgings for them. The family will consist of Mrs Hewitt, two young Ladies two Ladies maids & one man servant. I should suppose that a dinning [sic] room a bedchamber upon the same floor with or without a closet (but if a closet I should suppose rather better) with another bedchamber on the same floor or overhead for the young Ladies, & a room as near to them as may suit for the maids. Mrs Hewitt would like to lodge in one of the new houses of the Duke of Kingston where there is a bath in the house & I fancy that would be most convenient but as these baths in private houses have been made since I left Bath I could not give any certain advice, pray let me know how they are liked at Bath. I suppose Mrs Hewitt will be coming in about a fortnight & I wrote beforehand to ask your advice what you think will suit best & that Mrs Hewitt may have her choice of such Lodgings as are to be had. The more quiet and retired Mrs Hewitt's bedchamber is the better & her maids not too near & yet if anything should be wanting in the night within hearing of a bell. The more chearful the Lodgings are the better & especially the dining room. If you would be so good as to send us a line what choice you can meet with with number of rooms prices &c we should be much obliged to you; as to the other things that are necessary to be laid in upon coming to Bath that is more particularly in your way. Mr Hewitt does not come with Mrs Hewitt, but he may be very likely to come down for a few days & in that case I suppose he might have one additional room for his own use while he stays. I think we are never very scrupulous in giving you trouble but you will I am sure excuse it when I tell you that there is nothing that can interest all of us more than to accomodate Mrs Hewitt & family with the best reception that Bath can afford. We all join in best wishes to yourself Mrs Stennet and family.

7. The Cost of Living, 1775

There follows the accounts of Mr Richard Benyon of Englefield, Berkshire for part of September 1775 (Berkshire Record Office D/EBy A2). Comment on the life of a rich country gentleman of the period, using the evidence the accounts provide:

4	Dinner at Brentwood	4
5	Charity	4
6	E Wakelin, silversmith, on account	50
	Smiths Rat Book	5 6
7	P. Tolland, ¼ wages	3 10
	Andrew Baker, a bill	1 1 10
	Weights	5
	Ditto & Scales	5 6
	Sealing wax 4 lb	3 6
	At Footes Theatre	5
9	Worsted and Netting Needles	3
11	Park keeper	5
	Setting a Seal	7
	Map of the Seat of War	1 6
	Garord Tokeley, Carpenter	30 16 6
	John Kightley, Plumber	12 8
	William Pritchard, Plaisterer	4 14
	T. Watts, Glazier	12 3
	Cooke & Houghton, Painters	13 6
	Margaret Skeat, Bricklayer	1 1
12	M. Risdale, for a Black Man	19 19
	Mr Stuard	1 1
	Edward Hill, Mason	9 4
	Robson, Bookseller	8 19
	Stationary	1 6
	Carey Stafford, for Glass	1 7 6

147 19 1

8. Northern Ireland, 1798

Has anything changed in Northern Ireland? Read the following letter and consider how similar it is to the present situation, and in what ways it differs (Northern Ireland Public Record Office, D 607/1170).

I have to inform my Dear Lord of that with which I may safely conclude he is already acquainted – the impracticability, under the existing circumstances of this Country, of forming a Corps of Yeomanry Cavalry in this vicinity. The system of Terror – to borrow, or steal, a rascally tour d'exprorion – was never more completely organized under the Robespierrean Despotism than at this day in this part of Ireland. I am ever obtruding my notions, some more cruder &, may hap, some better concocted, but it is my opinion, grounded on *some* observation, that, in *these districts*, Yeomanry are not to be confided in, as a force of any tolerable efficiency. I am clear that the Fencible Regiments, to serve in the *British Islands,* would be more easily raised, more handily managed, more forceably & actively carried into military exertion than *Ulsterian* Yeomany. Numbers of idle fellows are now at large, numbers of manufacturers are turned loose, many of the United Dogs have been forceably imprised into the service of Rebellion – several have been seduced – not a few repent of the engagement – but of all the respective classes none dare enroll among the Yeomanry, and it might not consist altogether with the dictates of political caution to place much confidence in their service *in that line,* yet multitudes of them would enlist in the Fencible Regiment, & the Bounty is an argument of insinuating persuasion. I entertain little doubt that I could raise a Fencible Regiment in this Country, and, could I shake off some years, that heavily weigh down my energies of mind and body, I would propound my services – I *seriously* do not like the way we go on at present. In truth I do not see that we *get on.* This dis-armament I fear will be unproductive of intended effect – the military glean but few arms. I have had near forty Firelocks *voluntarily* brought in. I give receipts for the arms surrenderd, and I shall take Captain Marshall's receipt for all I give up to him. He is but little better than an oldGentlewoman.He was very *low* for a time, but since he has received reinforcements he grows *tall* apace.

I *really* am of the opinion that the *Farmers* in this part are well disposed, and wholly adverse to Insurgency, but they are intimidated, and the Rascality of the Country are wielded with much method, & with most profound secrecy of operation. The last Star, which by mere accident fell under my inspection sounds the Tocsin to Insurrection without any mufling whatever. If such treasonable publication cannot be punished, I must then say that the existing laws are wholly nugatory. A Presbyterian Parson, Porter of Grayabbey, has published a Sermon, for which, provided the proof of publication should not fail, I should think he might be handsomely trounced. These Fellows ought to be deprived of the Regnum Donum.They all, save two or three in the whole Province, are avowed Incendiaries.

When shall I have the pleasure to see General Lake I will take the liberty to intimate that, in his proclamation for disarming the Country, he ought to have excepted the Officers of Revenue.

    I have the Honour to be
        My Dear Lord
            Your Lordships most obliged
              and most gratefully devoted servant
                J Buckle
                15 March 1798

9. Swing Letter, 1830

This letter was sent to the Duke of Richmond during the 'Swing' riots. The Duke sent it on to the Prime Minister, no doubt as an example of what was going on. How responsible and sensible were the writers? (This letter is reproduced by kind permission of the Trustees of the Goodwood Collection.)

December 2 1830

Sir

We beg to say that if the sentences of the men in kent & all others for rioting is not reduseed to 3 months & all those taken heairafter to 1 monts ditto all the woods to a hedge stick on the duke of rishmans estaite with that of the other ministere the crown lands magestrates constabels & all engaged in takeing & triing the said men shall be all burnt up even to a furse bush but we promis faithfully if you comply with our request we will refrain from it What we want is Work & fair wages dont think that the reward will induse our men to split we have all put our hand to the match and we cannot betray each other and are determined to carry on and to set our starveing Countramen at liberty There is only 2 things to be done then we shall have peace & plenty that is machinery put down and the clergy paid out of the publick revenue and an income tax put on to take the abuse of the farmer in lieu of the tithes

10. House Plan

The plan below shows the ground floor of the house John Walter, the owner of The Times built for himself at Bearwood in Berkshire. Examine it with some care and see what conclusions you might draw from it about the way an early Victorian gentleman might want to have his house run.

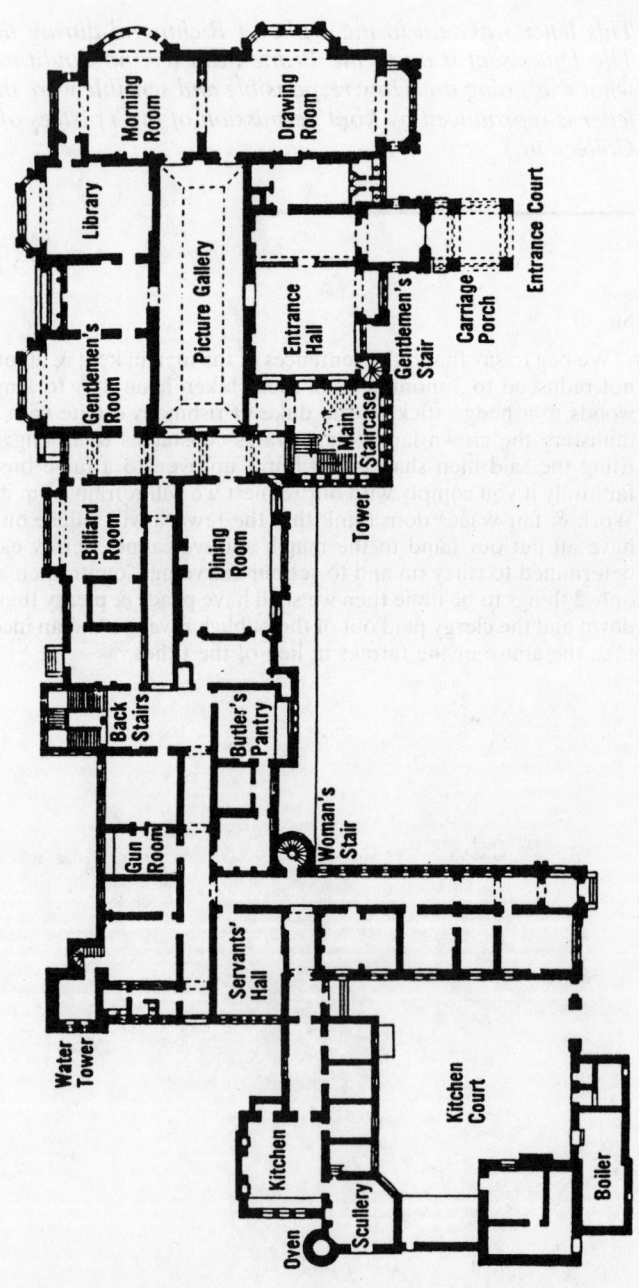

11. Rough Music, 1839

The following document consists of a file of case papers from the Walter archives (Berkshire Record Office D/EWl L3). In the light of the evidence presented, Mr John Walter has instructed his solicitors to take advice of Council as to whether a case might be brought and whether action would lie. Along with the case papers are two documents, an unsigned certificate and letter. The first document is very lengthy, and so is given in précis form; it is a request for counsel's opinion and is accompanied by the two documents which are given in full. The case did not come to court.

Although the story looks a simple and unimportant matter, there are at least three separate conflicts going on, not just the obvious one about William Goble's behaviour to his wife. Try to sort out the various interests in the affair. What do you think the 'rough musicians' believed they were doing, and why?

Document One: Précis of a Request for Counsel's Opinion

Mr William Goble has rented a cottage and a few acres of land in Hurst from Mr John Walter for some 8 to 9 years.The property divides two portions of the Simonds estate. The Simonds family are brewers long resident in Hurst, John Walter is the proprietor of The Times newspaper, newly resident at Bearwood, some three quarters of a mile from the Goble cottage.Two years previously he resigned as MP for the county as a result of misapprehension over his views on the Poor Law.

Goble's evidence: On August 17, 1839 Mr Goble quarrelled with his wife in consequence of her having been in a neighbour's house until 2 o'clock in the morning two or three nights previously. In the course of the quarrell he hit her two or three times with a thin stick. He spent the whole of Monday August 19th at Sonning on business, returning at 7 o'clock to find his wife very unwell, his son having fetched Dr Wheeler from Wokingham. Dr Wheeler deposed that Mrs Goble's illness was in no way connected with the beating she had received.

About 7.30 that evening some 16 or 18 men and boys assembled outside Goble's house equipped with horns, iron oven lids, pieces of iron, sheep bells, etc. They made a great deal of noise with these implements. At 8 o'clock Goble left the house to fetch medicine from Wokingham, as prescribed by Dr Wheeler, and was followed for about ¼ of a mile by the party, who continued to make 'rough music'which could be distinctly heard a mile away.Mr Goble spoke to them, saying "You're making a pretty good disturbance but not half noise eno' ", and then "I shall wish you good night." He observed William Mileham, David Miles and Henry Cooper to be of the party.

On Tuesday night some 25 to 30 people came similarly equipped and paraded up and down before the house making rough music until 9 o'clock. Mr Goble did not go out and therefore cannot identify those involved. The same was repeated on Wednesday.

The following Monday (August 26) some 30 people came at 8 and remained until between 9 and 10 o'clock. On Tuesday a similar group came at 8 and remained until 9.30, this time bringing a gun, which they shot at each turning point of their parade.

On Wednesday at least 40 arrived at 7 o'clock, as Mr Goble was leading his horse to the pond. David Miles said "Will you give me some beer now Master Goble?" receiving the reply "Yes, I shall think of you"; Miles replied "You will think of the rest as well as me, won't you?" Goble walked on a little and then said to William Mileham and Stephen White "I think this is complete rioting." Mileham said "I don't call it rioting," and Richard Chap said "This is always the rule when a man beats his wife." Goble replied "How do you know I beat my wife, Mr Wheeler is the best judge of that, he will satisfy you as to that."

The mob paraded for an hour, when Mr John Walter, accompanied by his friend Mr Austie and Robert Howard, the Bearwood gardener, and George Hill, Daniel Blake, John Eldridge, Richard Clark and Aaron Radburn, Bearwood servants, came to enquire the cause of the noise. Howard spoke to Goble, "You have got a pretty good row here why don't you stop it?" then, addressing the mob, asked them whether they meant to leave off. Stephen White replied 'No we shall keep on as long as we like." After an interval Howard spoke again "Now you had better drop it and go home quietly." Stephen White and William David replied "No we shan't, we are employed to do it." When Howard asked who employed them, someone said "thats no odds" and the mob continued to parade and rough music.

Howard and some of the Bearwood servants now seized some by their collars to try to make them go home. No blows were exchanged, but after half an hour's struggle the mob dispersed, Stephen White and William David saying "They had been there five nights and they should come another three and that would make eight nights." There were present William Millham, David Miles, Stephen White, William David, James May, John Blake, Henry Cooper, George Egerton and Richard Chap.

On Monday September 2 the mob returned at 7, and Robert Howard came down accompanied by James Poulter, Daniel Blake and Aaron Radburn. Howard sent for George Blake the Constable, but they refused to obey his order to disperse. They remained for two hours, among them being Stephen White, William David, William Mileham, David Miles, James May, John Oats, George Egerton, Thomas Radburn, Richard Chap, Henry Cooper, Samuel Mileham Junior and John Blake Junior.

On Tuesday 3 September only about 15 or 16 came, did not make much disturbance and soon went away. Goble said that he was at no time in fear. Robert Howard's evidence confirms that of William Goble (above) and adds the following list of people present in the rough music:

Stephen White, Groom to Mr Simonds; William David, Coachman to the same; Richard Chap, Gamekeeper to the same; John Oats, Miller to the same; James May, Labourer; John Blake, Sawyer; Charles Mosell, Labourer; William Benham, Labourer; James Cook, Labourer; William Cooper, Shoemaker; Thomas Radburn, Blacksmith; Samuel and William Mileham Carpenters; George Pain, George Egerton, James Woolridge, labourers; Robert Love, Bricklayer; John Blake Junior, Labourer.

Document Two: Certificate

"Certifieth

That on Wednesday August 28th between the hours of 7 and 9 in the evening, thirteen men with boys riotously assembled before Goble's house 5 of whom were known to be in service of Mr Symonds – 2 carrying blowers belonging to a grate of their Master's by their own confession, two other flags – on being requested by Mr. Howard to desist from the noise they were making said 'they did not care' – ' a friend would stand by them in case of being summoned before a Magistrate' – still continued walking up and down before the house, did so three times, would not give a reason for so doing, nor leave the spot until convinced that they could not force a way through those who appeared to be opposing them – The party with Mr Howard consisted of nine persons from Bearwood, used no violence, merely taking the men by the collar when words were found to be unavailing. Two flags were taken which were dropped in the road, not wrenched from the men."

Document Three: Unsigned Letter

"From a friend of good understanding, and not from a fool. Richard Clark you must not be surprised of a few lines to you from one who is not such a fool as yousel and all the rest of you. I suppose you thought you was going to frighten the Arborfield young men but you was devilish mistaken I wish they had given you a good ducking thats what licktrenchers ouht to have I have not been to interfere with the Bear Wood fools not yet but I shall be there on Monday to meet all the Cowards at the wood I will see that five fools shall not fall upon one Arborfield man to tread his toes and scratch his face. as for that bit of a Butler he looks like a tom tit upon a round of Beef and there is George Hill another such a fool and Radband the same. I wonder that you are not afraid the timber a falling upon you as you are cutting it but I suppose the other men are oblige to instruct you as they see you are such a fool some delight in having a fool as there is always one fool at the play so I reckon you as such.

so no more at present

a friend to truth and a looker on

I wrote it the postman brought it you paid for it law who woulda thought it

Peep fool peep peep at your brother why shant one fool peep at another I hope you will get served out for it you Coward youBear Wood Cowards I hope you will get a good ducking for it you bear wood fools O you cowards if I was your wife you should not have a bit of sugar in your tea I would put a turd in to see if that would sweeten it that would make it a Beautiful flavour."

12. The Poacher, 1847

This letter was written to Lord Northwick by one of his employees in 1847 (Worcester Record Office 705:66 BA 4221 – from the Lally and West collection). What does this letter reveal about the relationship between the two men?

Campden November 22 1847

My Lord I have the Liberty of Writing these few Lines to you in consequence of a notice I have received from Balinger the Keeper that I am Not to Cary a gun to kill squirils or rabits or any thing Else By your order my lord Balinger has been out in serch of Birds for 2 days and could not kill none and I herd you wanted some at the house the Next day I had the gun with me and I took the Liberty to kill 3 Birds and took them to the house Nor did i ever kill any thing wood Cocks or any thing but what i took to the house My Lord i have been a servent to you for six and twenty years and if any person can say i robed you of the worth of a peny i hope they will come forward to speak it to me face Before you i never did any thing but what your Lordship wished me to do since I carrid a gun i would not have killed the Birds if i had not known your Lordship wanted them this with evry other favour i have for your Lordship to Consider upon
Your Humble servent
William Cother
Campden

13. Train Times

Examine the two railway timetables given on the following pages and try to assess what has happened in the years that separate them. The first is from British Rail Western Region, the second from Berkshire Record Office D/ECb 02/5.

⇒ Bristol Temple Meads — Keynsham — Bath Spa

Mondays to Saturdays from 2 October to 12 May 1979

	Bristol Temple Meads	Keynsham	Bath Spa			Bristol Temple Meads	Keynsham	Bath Spa
MO	00 35	—	00 48			13 20	—	13 34
	03 50	—	04 03			13 50	—	14 01
	05 14	—	05 27			14 50	—	15 01
SX	06 20	—	06 31		D	15 10	—	15 21
D	06 50	—	07 01			15 15	—	15 29
	06 53	07 00	07 10			16 00	—	16 11
SX	07 15	—	07 26			16 10	16 17	16 29
D	07 45	—	07 56			16 30	—	16 41
	08 08	08 15	08 26			16 58	—	17 12
D	08 30	—	08 41		D	17 10	—	17 21
D	08 50	—	09 01			17 15	17 23	17 34
	09 10	—	09 21			17 40	—	17 51
	09 20	—	09 34			17 45	17 52	18 03
	09 50	—	10 01			18 40	—	18 51
	10 19	—	10 33		D	19 10	—	19 21
	10 50	—	11 01			19 15	—	19 29
D	11 10	—	11 21		G	20 10	—	20 21
	11 15	—	11 30			20 14	—	20 28
	11 50	—	12 01		D	21 10	—	21 21
SO	12 15	12 22	12 33			21 45	—	21 59
SX	12 19	—	12 33		H	23 05	—	23 19
	12 50	—	13 01		SO	23 05	—	23 40
D	13 10	—	13 21					

Notes
D   Through train from Weston-super-Mare
E   Through train to Weston-super-Mare
G   On Mondays to Fridays is a through train from Weston-super-Mare
H   Not Saturdays from 6 January
MO   Mondays only
MSO Mondays and Saturdays only
MSX Mondays and Saturdays excepted
FO   Fridays only
SO   Saturdays only
SX   Saturdays excepted
     By special bus (from 6 January)

BR35043/47 W308/1078

Awayday fares (2nd class)
Bristol T.M. to
Keynsham 55p
Bath Spa £1.03p
Keynsham to
Bath Spa 62p
Tickets must be purchased from the Guard on the train if passengers join at Keynsham or Oldfield Park
Save Money with a Season Ticket – Weekly, Monthly, Three Monthly and Annual tickets available. Prices on request. Ask for details of Sunday services.

⇒ Bath Spa — Keynsham — Bristol Temple Meads

Mondays to Saturdays from 2 October to 12 May 1979

	Bath Spa	Keynsham	Bristol Temple Meads			Bath Spa	Keynsham	Bristol Temple Meads
	00 28	—	00 45			15 41	—	15 56
MO	00 52	—	01 11			16 30	—	16 47
MSO	01 14	—	01 31		SX	17 05	17 16	17 24
MSX	01 23	—	01 39		E	17 15	—	17 32
	07 04	07 15	07 24		SX	17 35	—	17 52
SX	07 30	07 41	07 50		SO	17 41	—	17 58
SX	08 12	—	08 27			17 51	18 00	18 09
	08 19	08 30	08 38		SX E	18 07	—	18 24
SO	08 30	—	08 45		E	18 32	—	18 49
	08 45	—	09 00			18 39	—	18 54
E	09 15	—	09 32		E	19 16	—	19 33
	09 30	—	09 47			19 31	—	19 48
	09 47	—	10 02			19 41	—	19 56
	10 03	—	10 18			20 20	—	20 35
	10 31	—	10 48		FO	20 30	—	20 48
E	11 15	—	11 32		E	20 41	—	20 58
	11 24	—	11 39			21 47	—	22 04
	11 30	—	11 47		SO	21 53	—	22 10
	11 40	—	11 55			22 05	—	22 20
	12 30	—	12 47		H	23 15	—	23 32
	13 02	—	13 17		SO	23 59	—	00 25
E	13 15	—	13 32					
	13 30	—	13 47					
	14 30	—	14 47					
SX	14 40	—	14 55					
SO	14 40	14 51	15 00					
E	15 15	—	15 32					
	15 30	—	15 47					

The British Railways Board accept no liability for any inaccuracy in these tables which may be altered or cancelled at short notice, particularly at public holiday periods.

GREAT WESTERN RAILWAY.

N.B.—Coaches run from *Wootton Basset Road*, in connexion with the Railway, to Bath, Bristol, Bridgewater, Taunton, Exeter, Plymouth, Devonport, &c.; particulars of which may be obtained at the Stations, or the Company's usual Booking Offices.

Notice.—London Time is kept at all the Stations between *Paddington & Wootton Basset Road*, & will regulate the Arrivals & Departures. London Time is about 4 minutes earlier than the *Reading* time; 5 minutes & a half before *Steventon* time; 7 minutes & a half before *Wootton Basset Road* time; & the intermediate distances are in proportion thereto.

Horses & Carriages being at the Stations ten minutes before the time appointed for the departure of a Train, will be conveyed on this Railway. Four Horses are kept in readiness at the Stations; and upon sufficient notice being given to the Station-master, or the Bull and Mouth Office, St. Martin's-le-Grand, would be sent to bring Carriages from any part of London to the Station, at a charge of 5s. west of St. Martin's Lane, and 10s. 6d. beyond it, both including post boy.

Down Trains. (Daily, excepting Sundays.)

From Paddington to	Departure from Paddington	Ealing	Hanwell	Southall	West Drayton	Slough	Maidenhead	Twyford	Reading	Pangbourne	Goring	Wallingford Road	Steventon	Faringdon Road	Shrivenham	Arrival at Wootton Basset Road
Wootton Basset Rd. A.M.	8.0					8.35			9.13	9.26	9.34		9.59	10.17	10.34	10.53
Maidenhead	8.30	8.41	8.45	8.50	8.59	9.10										
Wootton Basset Road	9.0					9.35		10.3	10.15			10.39	10.59	11.16		11.50
Wootton Basset Road	10.0					10.35	10.47		11.15				11.57	12.14	12.31	12.50
Slough	10.30	10.41	10.45	10.50	10.59	11.10										
Wootton Basset Road	12.0				12.26	12.38	12.50	1.9	1.21	1.34		1.48	2.8	2.26		3.0
Slough .... P.M.	1.30	1.41	1.45	1.50	1.59	2.10										
Wootton Basset Road	2.0					2.35	2.47	3.5	3.17		3.37	3.44	4.1	4.19	4.36	4.53
Wootton Basset Road	2.0					4.35	4.47	5.5	5.17	5.30		5.44	6.3	6.21		6.55
Slough	4.30	4.41	4.46	4.50	4.59	5.10	5.20									
Reading	5.0		5.13		5.26	5.38	5.49	6.7	6.20							
Maidenhead	6.0	6.11	6.15	6.20	6.29	6.40	6.50									
Wootton Basset Road	8.0	8.11	8.16	8.20	8.29	7.35	8.53	9.12	8.13	8.25	8.33	8.41	9.1	9.19	9.36	
Reading	8.55				9.21	8.41	9.45		9.25							
W. Basset Rd. *Mail Train*						9.33			10.13			10.37	10.57	11.14		11.48
Goods' 4 o'clock A.M.	4.0			4.30	4.54	5.14	5.33	6.6	6.26	6.49		12.19	7.40	8.8		
Trains 9.30 „ P.M.	9.30					10.30			11.36				12.51	1.19	1.49	

Sunday Down Trains.

From Paddington to	Departure from Paddington	Ealing	Hanwell	Southall	West Drayton	Slough	Maidenhead	Twyford	Reading	Pangbourne	Goring	Wallingford Road	Steventon	Faringdon Road	Shrivenham	Arrival at Wootton Basset Road
Wootton Basset Rd. A.M.	8.0					8.36	8.48	9.7	9.19	9.32	9.39	9.46	10.6	10.23	10.41	11.0
Slough	8.30	8.41	8.46	8.52	9.2	9.15										
Reading	9.0				9.30	9.42	9.54	10.13	10.25							
Slough	9.30	9.42	9.48	9.20	10.2	10.15										
Wootton Basset Rd. P.M.	2.0	2.14		2.28	2.40	2.52		3.21	3.34		3.46	4.6	4.23	4.41	5.0	
Reading	2.0			5.32	5.45	5.58										
Slough	7.0	5.11	5.16	5.22	5.32	5.45	5.58	6.18	6.30	6.49						
W. Basset Rd. *Mail Train*	8.55	7.11	7.16	7.22	7.32	7.45	9.45		10.13			10.37	10.57	11.14		11.48

Up Trains, (Daily, excepting Sundays.)

UP — To Paddington from

To Paddington from	Departures from Wootton Basset Road	Shrivenham	Faringdon Road	Steventon	Wallingford Road	Goring	Pangbourne	Reading	Twyford	Maidenhead	Slough	West Drayton	Southall	Hanwell	Ealing	Arrival at Paddington
Wootton Basset Rd. a.m. (Mail Train)	2.30		3.1	3.18	3.36			4.0		4.29	4.40	4.52				5.20
Reading								7.30	7.39	7.56	8.6	8.18	8.28	8.33	8.38	8.50
Slough											9.0	9.10	9.19	9.24	9.28	9.40
Maidenhead										9.50	10.0	10.10	10.19	10.24	10.28	10.40
Wootton Basset Road	8.30	8.47	9.3	9.19	9.37	9.46		10.6	10.19	10.37	10.49					11.26
Reading								11.0		11.25	11.35	11.47	11.57	12.3	12.8	12.20
Wootton Basset Road	10.15	10.32	10.48	11.6	11.23			11.47	12.0		12.27					1.—
Wootton Basset Road	11.30		12.1	12.18		12.42	1.50	1.2		1.31	1.42					2.20
Slough											3.0	3.10	3.19	3.24	3.28	3.40
Wootton Basset Rd. p.m.	1.15	1.32	1.49		2.24			2.49			3.31					4.—
Wootton Basset Road	2.30		3.2	3.19			3.49	4.2		4.30	4.43					6.20
Slough											6.0	6.10	6.19	6.24	6.28	6.40
Wootton Basset Road	4.30	4.47	5.2	6.19	5.37	6.46		6.4	6.17	6.35	7.54					7.20
Maidenhead										7.46	8.35	8.6	8.16	8.22	8.27	8.40
Wootton Basset Road	6.30	7.16	7.0	7.16			7.46	7.58				7.9				9.10
Goods' Trains { 3 o'clock a.m.	3.0		3.57	4.24	4.55		9.13	5.38	9.59	6.30	6.46	7.9				8.0
6.45 p.m.	6.45	7.16	7.45	8.14	8.47			9.33			10.45		11.35			11.08

Sunday Up Trains.

To Paddington from	Departures from Wootton Basset Road	Shrivenham	Faringdon Road	Steventon	Wallingford Road	Pangbourne	Reading	Twyford	Maidenhead	Slough	West Drayton	Southall	Hanwell	Ealing	Arrival at Paddington
Wootton Basset Rd. a.m. (Mail Train)	2.30		3.1	3.18	3.36		4.0	7.39	4.29	4.40	4.52				5.—
Reading							7.30		7.56	8.6	8.18	8.28	8.33	8.38	8.50?
Slough										9.0	9.10	9.19	9.24	9.28	9.40
Wootton Basset Rd. p.m.	2.0	2.17	2.34	2.49	3.8	3.22	3.34	3.48	4.7	4.18	5.10	5.21	5.28	7.1	5.45
Slough										5.0	6.40		6.55		7.15
Wootton Basset Road	5.0	5.17	5.34	5.49	6.8	6.24	6.36	6.50	7.9	7.21	7.34	9.3	9.10	9.16	8.—
Reading							8.0		8.27	8.39	8.52				
Goods' Trains { 3 o'clock a.m.	3.0		3.57	4.24	4.55	9.13	5.38	9.59	6.30	6.46	7.9	11.35			
6.45 p.m.	6.45	7.16	7.45	8.14	8.47		9.33			10.45					11.08

Passengers and Parcels, between the long and short Stations, can proceed in either direction to Slough, and be taken on by the succeeding Train.

FARES.

Children under TEN Years of Age are charged Half Price.

Paddington to	First Class	Second Class Open Carriage	Goods Trains	Carriages 4-Wheel	Carriages 3-Wheel	Horses Each	Horses For Pair being the same Property
Ealing							
Hanwell							
Southall							
West Drayton							
Slough							
Maidenhead							
Twyford							
Reading							
Pangbourne							
Goring							
Wallingford Road							
Steventon							
Faringdon Road							
Shrivenham							
Wootton Basset Rd							

Wootton Basset Road to	First Class	Second Class Open Carriage	Goods Trains	Carriages 4-Wheel	Carriages 3-Wheel	Horses Each	Horses For Pair being the same Property
Shrivenham							
Faringdon Road							
Steventon							
Wallingford Road							
Goring							
Pangbourne							
Reading							
Twyford							
Maidenhead							
Slough							
West Drayton							
Southall							
Hanwell							
Ealing							
Paddington							

The Goods Train Passengers will be conveyed in uncovered Trucks by the Goods Trains only, and 14-lbs. of Luggage allowed for each.

The Charge for Goods between Paddington and the Wootton Basset Road Station, will be 23s. per Ton; and between Paddington and Reading, 12s. per Ton, including loading and unloading. The Charge to the other Stations is in proportion. Sheep, Beasts, &c., are conveyed by the Goods' Trains.

Coaches will run between Wootton Basset Road Station and Bath, a distance of 30 miles; the Faringdon Road Station and Cheltenham, Stevenson Station and Oxford, through Abingdon; between the Twyford Station and Henley; the Maidenhead Station and Marlow and Wycombe; the West Drayton Station and Uxbridge; and Windsor Omnibuses meet every Train at Slough.

Omnibuses start from Princes Street, Bank, one hour before the departure of each Train, calling at the Angel Inn, Islington; Bull Inn, Holborn; Moore's Green Man & Still, Griffin's Green Man & Still, Oxford Street; Goldcn Cross.

Charing Cross; Chaplin's Universal Office, and Bull & Mouth, Regent Circus; and Gloucester Warehouse, Oxford Street, to the Paddington Station, Fare Sixpence, without Luggage.

Parcels may be booked at the Railway Offices, Princes Street, Bank, and Paddington; at the Coach Offices, Spread Eagle, Gracechurch Street, & Regent Circus; the Bull & Mouth, St. Martin's le Grand, & Regent Circus; Golden Cross, Charing Cross & Regent Circus; Griffin's Green Man & Still, & Moore's Green Man & Still, Oxford Street; Bull Inn, Holborn; George & Blue Boar, Holborn, Angel Inn; Clemens, & Islington; Swan with two Necks, Lad Lane; Cross Keys, Wood Street, White Horse, Fetter Lane; Hatchett's White Horse Cellar, Piccadilly, the Western Office, corner of Portman Street, for Bristol, & all parts of the West of England, & the Towns & Villages right & left of the Line of Railway, at which places & at the Stations they will also be received for Conveyance. Two Daily Deliveries will be made in London.

BRISTOL AND BATH.

HOURS OF DEPARTURE, Regulated by Bristol Time, until the whole Line shall be Opened, Daily, (excepting Sundays.)

UP From Bristol	Departure from				Arrives at
To BATH A.M.	BRISTOL	KEYNSHAM	SALTFORD	TWERTON	BATH
	h. m.	h. m.	h. m.	h. m.	h. m.
To BATH A.M.	7.0	8.40		8.51	7.23
"	8.30		9.45		8.56
"	9.30	11.40	1.46	11.51	9.55
"	11.30	1.40			11.56
P.M.	1.30			2.50	1.56
"	2.30	3.40			2.55
"	3.30		4.45		3.55
"	4.30	5.40			4.55
"	5.30		6.45	6.51	5.55
"	6.30	8.40			6.56
"	8.30				8.30

DOWN From Bath	Departure from				Arrives at
To BRISTOL A.M.	BATH	TWERTON	SALTFORD	KEYNSHAM	BRISTOL
	h. m.	h. m.	h. m.	h. m.	h. m.
To BRISTOL A.M.	8.0	9.24	8.10	8.16	8.26
"	9.30				9.55
"	10.30			10.45	10.55
"	12.30		12.40	12.46	12.56
P.M.	2.30	2.34			2.55
"	3.30			3.45	3.55
"	4.30		4.40		4.55
"	5.30	5.34		5.46	5.56
"	6.30		6.40		6.55
"	7.30				7.53
"	9.30				9.56

ON SUNDAYS,

	A. M.		h. m. 8.0	h. m. 9.0	h. m. 9. 4	h. m. 10.0	h. m. 10.10	h. m. 9.16	h. m. 9.26
	"		9.0	10.0		3.30	3.42	3.48	10.26
	P.M.		2.30	3.34	3.42	6.30	6.42	6.48	4. 0
	"		5.30	6.34	6.42	9.30	9.42	9.48	7. 0
	"		8.30	9.34	9.42				10. 0

UP From Bristol

	First Class	Second Class	CARRIAGE, Four-Wheel	Two-Wheel	HORSES Each	For Pair, being the same Property
To Keynsham ..	1	0				
" Saltford	2	3				
" Twerton	2	6				
" Bath			8 0	6 0	7 0	12 0

FARES.

DOWN From Bath

	First Class	Second Class	CARRIAGE, Four-Wheel	Two-Wheel	HORSES Each	For Pair, being the same Property
To Twerton ..	1	0				
" Saltford	2	6				
" Keynsham ..	2	6				
" Bristol ..			8 0	6 0	7 0	12 0

The undermentioned Coaches are in connexion with the Railway.—No Fees are allowed to Coachmen or Guards.

UP.

(coach timetable listing coaches including White Lion, Bristol; Bush; York House; White Hart; etc.)

DOWN.

(coach timetable)

UP. On Sundays.

DOWN.

Fares by Railway & Coaches

		Inside			Outside			
Bristol, to or from Paddington Station	Ditto							
Bath	Ditto							
Melksham ..	Ditto							
Chippenham ..	Ditto							
Devizes	Ditto							
Calne	Ditto							
Taunton (by Bristow)	Ditto							
Bridgwater,	Ditto							
Glastonbury	Ditto							
Wells ..	Ditto							
Shepton Mallet	Ditto							

Parcels.

W. Snell, Printer, &c, Newcastle Place, Edgware Road, London.—February 16, 1841.

14. Slavery Observed, 1853

William Makepeace Thackeray, the famous English novelist went on a lecture tour of the USA in 1853. He wrote home to his 13 year old daughter from South Carolina, commenting on the issue of slavery. He included a portrait, opposite; extracts from his letter are transcribed below.

How useful would you find Thackeray's evidence in assessing the problem of slavery in the Southern States of the USA in the years leading up to the Civil War?

March 11 Charleston. S Carolina

My dearest Finikin. Isn't it your turn to have a letter? Here is a page with a picture already done on it of a young lady who sells pea-nuts and whom Eyre [Eyre Crowe, Thackeray's secretary] brought home the other day when she was so good as to sit for her portrait. What interests one in this place is the negro children I think. I am never tired of watching their little queer half pretty half funny faces. It's a great error to suppose they are unhappy, they are the merriest race ever seen & they are tended by their masters with uncommon care. They have the best of food, of doctors when they are ill, of comfortable provision in old age. Slaves they are and that's wrong: but admitting that sad fact, they are the best cared for poor that the world knows of. Eyre and I went to a black ball the other night. It was such queer melancholy fun! The men danced capitally, they are house servants in the town mostly, as grave & polite as if they had been noblemen. But the women were preternaturally hideous all of them and dressed in such white frocks with tiaras and feathers and white saten shoes (a few) and black scraggy shoulders and arms showing so queer in the white dresses. Not one of them to compare with the pretty pea-nut girl with her slim figure and sweet voice...I wish you could have seen the little nigger who sang a song for us last night in the street! a little imp of two feet high who sang the song of the Figlia del Regimento to nigger words of his own!It was quite surprising to hear the sweetness of the child's voice. Yesterday at dinner I felt my elbow scratched and looking there I saw a little negro with a bread basket offering to me. His master says the child hits him sometimes in the back to make him attend. At most of the tables there are a couple of these pretty little imps with great peacock fans brushing the flies away – that is the first part of household duty which they learn. The ladies of a family universally wash their won teacup after breakfast. Each slave only does one set of duties – the washerwoman for instance does nothing but wash, & has a little black girl to help her, the cook has a kitchen maid, and so on: besides it being wrong slavery is 6 times as dear as free labour. People having 12 servants to do what 2 will do in England...

To sell and shell peanuts is Margaret's occupation
She makes foo dollars a day often at this trade - not for
herself but for her mistress. Margaret is free. She dono
how old she is thinks about 16. She earns 5 dollars
a month wages. She goes to
Bethels chapel Methodists.
She wears a silk frock Sundays,
do noo what colour frock sorta grey
earrings and a bonnet - a blue
bonnet and blue ribbons inside
She can't write but she can read
a little - not so as to
amuse her
self - any read.
She has heard
of England:
not much
only that
it is a
fine place
She
made
her
own
Jacket
She can
. sing: but she
has never been to the play. She laughs: Coloured people ain't allowed to go
Margaret says. She has no sweetheart - never had one Margaret says.

15. The Victoria Cross

*The following items relating to the Victoria Cross come from The Times,
26 February 1980 and 6 November 1980. The pawn ticket itself is at the
Royal Hampshire Regiment Museum, Winchester, and is reproduced
here by kind permission of the Trustees. Consider what light they cast
upon the place of military prowess and individual courage in nineteenth
and twentieth century British History.*

£8,800 paid for posthumous Victoria Cross

By Geraldine Norman
Sale Room Correspondent

Horace Waller was 20 years old
in 1917 when he displayed such
conspicuous gallantry in throwing
bombs at his German enemies
against fearful odds that he won
a Victoria Cross. It cost him his
life. His posthumous VC was sold
at Christie's yesterday for £8,800
to Spink's (estimate £8,000-
£9,000).

Christie's catalogue records that
Mr Waller joined the Army as a
private in 1916 after being twice
rejected on medical grounds. He
served with the King's Own York-
shire Light Infantry.

His old school magazine at Bat-
ley Grammar School wrote of him:
" Few of his chums suspected
that his staid and peaceful frame
concealed the spirit of the man
who should bring the school its
greatest honour on the field ".
Heroism today is reflected in high
prices.

Christie's sale of banknotes and
medals totalled £41,978, with 4 per
cent unsold. A Chinese imperial
government gold loan bond of
1898, expected to be one of the
most costly rarities, was withdrawn from the sale

At Sotheby's a sale of French
and other glass paperweights made
£84,611, with 3 per cent unsold.
As predicted, a St Louis cruci-
form, carpet-ground weight made
the top price at £5,000 (estimate
£5,000-£6,000). It went to Schull,
an American dealer, who also paid
£4,200 (estimate £3,000-£4,000) for

a very fine Clichy moss-ground
weight with a pink and white in-
terlaced trefoil.

Sotheby's sale of printed books
was almost a sell-out, totalling
£24,374, with less than half of 1
per cent unsold. Braun and
Schmidt, book dealers from West
Germany, paid the top price of
the day at £1,350 (estimate £600-
£800) for an early printing,
Schedel's *Liber Cronicorum* (298
leaves only), published in Augs-
burg in 1497.

The sad tale of Gunner Collis, VC and bars

A Victoria Cross, won in Afghanistan exactly a century ago and subsequently reclaimed by the War Office because its holder was found to be a bigamist, comes up for auction at Sotheby's later this month after army museum interests failed to have it taken off the market.

Few medals can have had such a chequered career as this one. But it is expected to fetch only between £5,500 and £6,500, far below the record price at auction for a VC of £17,000; despite its curous history it is an early issue, when the award was handed out a good deal less discriminately than in later years.

Gunner James Collis, of the Royal Horse Artillery, a Cambridge man, won it for conspicuous bravery in the retreat from Maiwand during the Second Afghan War in 1880 and had it pinned on his chest by Lord Roberts on Poona racecourse. In 1895 Collis was arrested on a charge of bigamy and convicted; the War Office demanded the medal back but, as Collis had pawned it, they had to redeem it from the pawnshop with government money.

Queen Victoria had stipulated that any holder of the medal who was later convicted of a crime had to be struck off the register. The decision was reversed by George V, who decreed that all forfeited VCs should be returned to their holders, but by that time not only had Collis died but the War Office had lost his medal.

It was not seen again until 1938, when it turned up at an auction and was bought by a Colonel Oakley. Last year John Oakley, a London patent agent, disposed of his father's medal collection at auction and the VC was bought by Spinks, the London dealers.

But its strange career was not yet over.

The Ogilby Trust, which represents a number of army museums, immediately objected to the sale on the grounds that, as the medal had been confiscated and never returned to Collis, it was Crown property. Spinks had to give it back.

Whereupon learned counsel were engaged and spent much time (and probably a great deal of their clients' money) debating the issue. They eventually decided that the medal was not Crown property, the Ministry of Defence concurred, and Oakley has now been given full clearance to put it on sale again.

Between the introduction of the VC in 1856 and George V's decree that wrongdoers should not have their gongs confiscated, a total of eight VCs were forfeited. Considering the history and the low estimate put on poor Collis's, it seems an absolute snip.

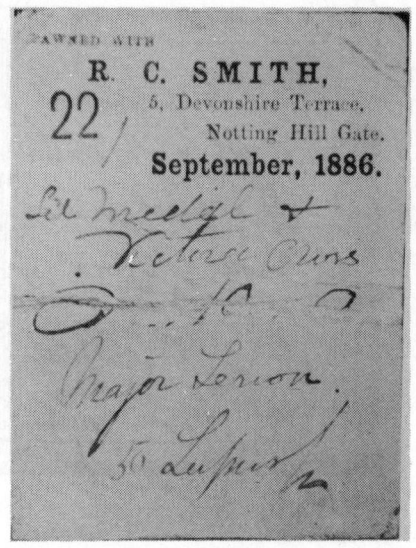

16. The Water Bottle, 1880

The poor leave few records, so what we have has a rarity value. What evidence does this example have to offer to the historian of the English working classes? From F. Atkinson, The Great Northern Coalfield, 1700-1900, *University Tutorial Press, 1968, p. 43.*

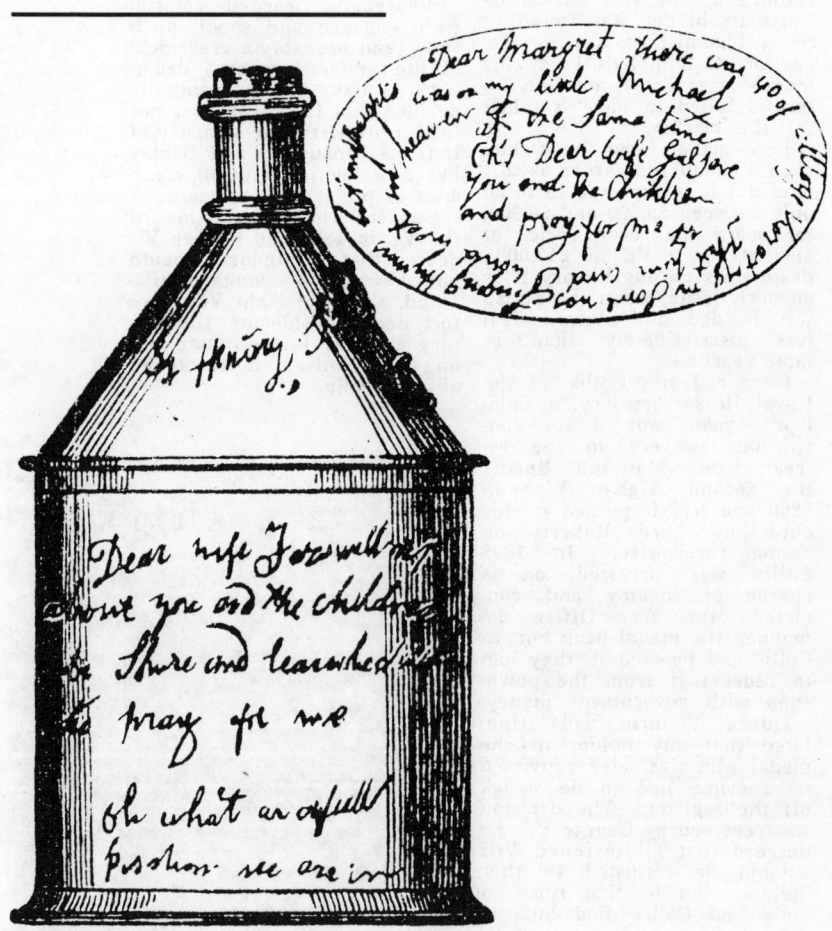

Fig. 33. A LAST MESSAGE SCRATCHED WITH A NAIL ON A TIN WATER-BOTTLE. SEAHAM EXPLOSION. 1880. The message reads:

Dear Margaret.

There was 40 of us altogether at 7 a.m. Some was singing hymns, but my thoughts was on my little Michael that him and I would meet in heaven at the same time. Oh Dear wife, God save you and the children, and pray for me . . . Dear wife Farewell. My last thoughts are about you and the children. Be sure and learn the children to pray for me. Oh what an awful position we are in.

Michael Smith. 54 Henry Street.

(From *Explosion in Coal Mines*, W. N. and J. B. Atkinson, 1886.)

17. Letter about an Airman, 1916

What sort of problems did parents and officers face in the First World War? Read the document given below (Berkshire Record Office D/Ex23 F30/1) and try to envisage these two parties, rather than the one who was lost.

No: 70 Squadron,
R.F.C.
B.E.F.

3.11.1916

Dear Mr. Nicholson,

By the time you get this I expect you will have had a wire from the War Office telling you that your Son was missing on the 31st of October.

I am very sorry to have to send you such bad news.

He went out on a patrol in the afternoon with five other machines, to patrol the area round Bapaume. They only met one German machine, and really had no proper fighting. Owing to the leaders engine failing and causing him to land the patrol became rather split up, and when they returned none of them knew very much what had happened to the remainder during the last part of the time. They were rather heavily shelled over Bapaume but none of them saw any machine brought down.

I have received no reports from anywhere of any machine being brought there that day, and it seems very extraordinary that your Son did not return.

I suppose that his engine must have failed, or been hit, and that he was forced to land.

He may of course have been hit himself, but I do not see any more reason for thinking that than the opposite. I hope that you will hear before very long that he is safe though a Prisoner.

The news usually takes a month to six weeks to get through and nearly always comes in the form of a letter or P.Card home from the Prisoner.

I am extremely sorry to lose him. He had not been with the Squadron very long, but he had already done good work and shown his keenness and ability.

He was an exceptional pilot and would very soon have got his flight.

We shall all miss him very much.

I have had his Kit packed up and it is being forwarded to you via Cox's Shipping Agency, Charing Cross, London.

It takes a long time to arrive I am afraid. Perhaps as much as six weeks.

If there is any more I can do please let me know.

If I should hear anything I will of course let you know, but we hardly ever get news out here.

I should be much obliged if you would let me know if you hear anything. We are always so anxious to know.

Yours sincerely,

(SGD:) J.A.K. Lawrence,

Major

18. A Welcome for Mussolini, 1923

The following poem, praising the new regime of Mussolini (who had marched on Rome the previous October) appeared in the Wall Street Journal in January 1923 (and was reprinted in a review in The Times Literary Supplement, 2 March 1973). What is it that the author likes about the new regime? What does he hope for from it? What interests and fears does the author represent? It would be useful for you to look into a chronology of History for this period to find out what was happening in Europe and America in these months – it would help you to answer more effectively (Neville Williams's Chronology of The Modern World, 1763-1965, *Penguin Books, 1975, is a most useful example).*

On constitutional technique
And precedents he's lame,
On grace and glamour rather weak
Such lacks don't cramp his game!
Instead they're assets for his job,
Rough, rude, plain word and act,
To mould a nation through a mob,
To make a dream a fact!
Red nonsense had its mischief proved;
His black-shirts curbed and quelled,
Perhaps in ways not graced or grooved,
How the reins be held?
A blacksmith's son to purple Rome
A brusque command he brought;
Italia, cleansed and rescued home
But more than her he's taught
Word-froth and demagogues and drones
Banned; sweat and service praised;
Desks manned when A.M. intones,
Languorous Italy dazed!

19. The General Strike

How far can personal, private documents be used to illuminate the great political events of state? Use the following letters and attempt an answer based on this material. Letters from a gentleman in London to his wife convalescing in Switzerland, describing the General Strike of 1926. Personal matter is excised (Berkshire Record Office D/EX 239).

7th May
...the position is unchanged. The Govt. will not reopen negotiations until the general strike notices are withdrawn and the T.U.C refuse to withdraw them.

I have not been able to get a paper today though I read a fly sheet DailyTelegraph stuck on a shop window.There was not much in it except a statement that there was a certain amount of disorder in the Eastern Districts of Northern England Edinburgh, Aberdeen and that some food lorries had been stopped leaving Southampton.

I think the T.U.C is genuinely anxious to avoid disaster but it will be increasingly unable to prevent hooligans mostly young who may not beTrades Union members at all from beginning to wreck things. It is a fact that a few buses and cars have been wrecked trying to drive through S.E. London yesterday evening. I got a lift this morning from Belsize Park in a car which dropped people off at Notting HillGate and S. Kensington before going to Westminster, so I had a good round during which there was no sign of any disorder. We were held up for about ¼ of an hour while a stream of empty lorries left Hyde Park. General buses are running with a policeman on the box beside the driver and barbed wire on the bonnet.

Passenger transport is greatly improved. I got home by tube from Leicester Sq. to Belsize Park yesterday evening, leaving the office just after 4, the train was not even crowded! The Tube, Met & District services will be something approaching normal today while all the railways are able to run mail trains.In fact *at the moment* as far as *passenger* transport is concerned I think one could fairly say that the rly strike was a failure, though of course there is delay and crowding. No goods or coal trains are being run. I wish I knew how much coal there is above ground and what the prospects are of being able to move it from the pit mouth. Nothing is rationed yet. It is an offence to buy more than 1 cwt of coal a week but how people are to be stopped going to different coalmerchants I do not know. ...wants to buy a oil cooker etc but I have discouraged her so far, partly because I think panicking is to be deprecated, and also if things got to the stage when gas and electricity supplies for domestic use cannot be maintained, there will be no food either, and I am not prepared to lay in a store of food.

Later. I have got todays 'British Gazette'. Don't pay any attention to wild rumours that appear in the Continental Daily Mail or foreign papers. I have arranged with...to drive me to the office every day!

13th May
Today's Times has real interest, and I send yesterdays and the T.U.C. sheet announcing the end. I do not know what was the deciding factor in making the T.U.C. throw up the sponge and let down the miners. I can only imagine that they came to the conclusion that the General Strike was beginning to fail, as indeed I suppose it was. The pretext that there is anything new in Samuels memorandum beyond what was in the Coal Commission Report is too flimsy for

words, as is seen by its immediate rejection by the miners. I did overhear someone at the 1917 club say that Ashbury's judgement has 'put the wind up' the T.U.C. If it is good law its consequences about the illegality of strike pay etc. are highly important, because there are enough dissentients in all the Unions to raise Cain and there would have been injunctions flying all over the place and any dissentient Trades Union members could have made T.U.C. Executives personally responsible for all strike pay disbursed.I must say it was a surprise to me that there was anything illegal about a sympathetic strike. If there is, the Labour Party when they come into office at the next General Election, will soon alter the law and quite rightly. You will find Ashbury's judgement in the Times of Wednesday. I expect he was got at by the Govt. It reads too much like some of the war judgements which were obviously bad law.

The shorthand notes of the interview between Baldwin and the T.U.C. were broadcast last night. Frightfully interesting but quite unprecedented to publish that sort of thing at all. I hope the Govt. got the T.U.C. permission, though all the speeches were so good on behalf of the T.U.C. that I do not think that any of the speakers will be harmed by the publication. I think Baldwin should have made a great deal stronger appeal to employers to reinstate strikers. I am afraid there will be an appalling amount of victimisation by employers.

The coal strike position remains as it was – hopeless.

After lunch. Very few strikers have gone back to work. They demand unconditional reinstatement en masse. There will be serious trouble unless the Govt. makes employers take men back, and every effort should be concentrated on that. The position is a very difficult one, as the dislocation has been so serious that even with the best will in the world many employers will be hard put to it to pay their men if they do take them back, while many employers will want to victimise. It is desperate.

Monday 17th May

I send you the latest strike Times. We are promised ordinary papers tomorrow.The general strikers are going back to work in a way I thought very unlikely at one time. Things looked very bad on Thursday until Baldwin's speech to the House became generally known. Ordinary trains are going back again, though the service is only about 50% of the full one, but this is owing to the coal shortage, not men shortage. It took just under 4 hours to get to Cambridge on Saturday, the train stopping at all stations. This morning one of the ordinary expresses was running, doing the journey in under the hour and a half.

They were all well at Cambridge, poor...minding the collapse of the strike frightfully, and what she calls the bootlicking attitude of the T.U.C. Ramsay etc. Apparently nearly all the undergraduates went down during the strike and became specials or volunteers of some sort. I dined at High Table in Trinity next to a Fellow who had been in charge of 600 undergraduate specials who were barracked in a Water Closet warehouse in Whitechapel and did nothing except practice 'embusments' they being shocktroops ready to be sent anywhere in London. It all sounds very military but they were not used.

I wined next the Master and went round to the lodge afterwards. I remained quite sober and thoroughly enjoyed it. Housman was there, a rather pathetic figure I thought, obviously the most outstanding personality, but frightfully shy and quiet and looking dreadfully unhappy. ...says he does not think he allows anyone to be intimate with him.

Now that the general strike is over I do not mind telling you that I found it a great strain, waiting for the worst, all by myself! I have not minded anything so much since the beginning of the war.I am glad you were out of it.

20. A Family Portrait

Read the following letter from a father to his daughter who is away on holiday and look at the picture of the writer's mother. From these two sources, what might one say about the writer? Write your answer before turning over to the next page.

'Little Housekeeper:

I got your letter and postcard. I'm glad you haven't forgotten your little papa. I'm sending you a few red apples. In a few days I'll send tangerines. Eat them and enjoy yourself. I'm not sending Vasya any because he's doing badly in school. The weather is nice here. Only, I'm lonely because my little Housekeeper isn't with me. All the best, then, my little Housekeeper, I give you a big kiss.

October 8th, 1934

The subject of this exercise was Josef Stalin, pictured here. In January 1935 he had initiated the first 'treason trials' in which he was to carry out the most massive persecution of his enemies and of those he believed to be his enemies. Do you want to change what you have already written, or do you want to change your view of Stalin the persecuter? The picture of Stalin's mother appeared in For all the World to See: the Life of Margaret Bourke-White, *edited by Johnathan Silverman, and is reproduced by kind permission of Margaret Bourke-White/Life (c) Time Inc. the letter is from* Twenty Letters to a Friend *by Svetlana Alliluyeva (1967), and is reproduced by kind permission of Svetlana Alliluyeva and the Hutchinson Group Limited.*

Other Publications in this series which are particularly relevant:

TH34,
The Development of Thinking and The Learning of History,
by Jeanette B. Coltham

TH35,
Educational Objectives for the Study of History: a suggested framework,
by Jeanette B. Coltham in collaboration with John Fines

both available from the Historical Association, 59a Kennington Park Road, London SE11 4JH, or telephone your order on 01-735 3901 using your Credit Card (answerphone outside office hours)

Other Publications in this series include:

TH44,
The New History: theory
into practice,
by P. J. Rogers

TH55,
A Survey of A-Level History,
by John Fines

both available from the Historical
Association, 59a Kennington Park Road,
London SE11 4JH, or telephone your order
on 01-735 3901 using your Credit Card
(answerphone outside office hours)